arco notes

WILLIAM SHAKESPEARE'S

Julius Caesar

by DAVID R. TURNER, M.S. *in ED.*

New York

Printed in the United States of America

Library of Congress
Catalog Card Number: 75-82575

Standard Book Number 668-01984-0

For information about this work, and about other
ARCONOTES, please write to:
Arco Publishing Company, Inc.
219 Park Avenue South
New York, N. Y. 10003

CONTENTS

JULIUS CAESAR

List of Characters in *Julius Caesar*

Julius Caesar, Dictator of Rome
Cassius, Originator of the plot to kill Caesar
Marcus Brutus, Friend of Caesar

THE THREE RULERS AFTER CAESAR'S MURDER

Octavius Caesar, Julius Caesar's grandnephew
Marcus Antonius (Marc Antony), Caesar's loyal friend
M. Aemilius Lepidus, A great general

SENATORS

Cicero, Publius, Popilius Lena

OTHER MEMBERS OF THE PLOT AGAINST JULIUS CAESAR

Trebonius, Ligarius, Decius Brutus, Metellus Cimber, Cinna, Casca

TRIBUNES OF THE PEOPLE

Flavius, Marullus

SUPPORTERS OF BRUTUS AND CASSIUS

Lucilius, Titinius, Messala, Young Cato, Volumnius, Varro, Clitus, Claudius, Strato, Lucius, Dardanius

OTHER CHARACTERS

Artemidorus, teacher of speech

A Soothsayer (fortune teller)

Cinna, a poet

Another Poet

Pindarus, Cassius' servant

Calpurnia, Caesar's wife

Portia, Brutus' wife

Caesar's Ghost

Servant to Caesar; Marc Antony; Octavius

Senators, citizens, guards, attendants, etc., etc.

Brief Summary of the Play

The play opens, and we see a group of Roman citizens waiting to cheer Caesar's return from a military victory over a former ally, Pompey. Flavius and Marullus, supporters of Pompey, chide the crowd for forgetting a former hero, Pompey, in favor of Caesar.

Caesar enters with a large following. A fortune teller warns him to beware the 15th of March. Cassius, meanwhile, tells Caesar's friend, Brutus, that he hates Caesar, and tries to enlist Brutus in a plot to overthrow Caesar. Caesar leaves. Later, we learn that Antony, a friend of Caesar, has tried three times to persuade Caesar to become king. Although Caesar refuses, Brutus is troubled that he will change his mind and become a dictator. Casca, another enemy of Caesar, agrees to join the plot.

The night before the Ides of March, during a storm, we learn from Casca that the plotters have decided to kill Caesar. Cassius explains it is necessary to win Brutus over to the cause.

Brutus, on the same evening, is debating with himself what course of action to take. Finally, he decides that Caesar must die. At the same time he makes his decision, the other conspirators in the plot arrive—Cassius, Casca, Decius Brutus, Cinna, Metellus Cimber and Trebonius. They agree to kill Caesar the next day, for it is rumored that the Senate of Rome

1

will offer Caesar the throne at the Capitol where they meet. Brutus' wife enters after the plotters have left, and demands an explanation of why her husband is so worried these last few days. Brutus is about to explain when still another plotter, Ligarius, arrives.

During the same stormy night, Caesar cannot sleep. His wife, Calpurnia, troubled by dreams of Caesar's assassination, begs him to remain at home. Caesar pooh-poohs his wife's fears. He asks the priests to sacrifice an animal and tell his fortune. The priests comply, and tell Caesar that the gods advise he not go out. Caesar is convinced he should not venture out, but when one of the plotters, Decius Brutus, arrives and chides him for cowardice, Caesar relents. Against the advice of the priests and the pleas of his wife, Caesar leaves for the Capitol on the Ides of March.

While Caesar is being escorted by a number of the conspirators, Artemidorus, a teacher of speech, tries to slip him a letter warning him of the conspiracy. Caesar will not listen.

Caesar's friend Marc Antony is called away by one of the plotters so he cannot save Caesar in the Capitol. Then the murderers kill Caesar.

When Antony returns to view the body of Caesar, he swears revenge. He convinces Brutus to allow him to deliver the funeral oration, promising that he will not say anything nasty about the plotters. But, in his speech, he whips

BRIEF SUMMARY

the crowd up into a fury by reading Caesar's will. The will, it turns out, gives all of Caesar's wealth to the common people. Naturally, these common people are enraged against the plotters. They run wild, burn the houses of the plotters, and drive Brutus, Cassius and the others out of Rome. Antony, and a nephew of Caesar named Octavius who has just arrived, join up with Lepidus and take over Rome.

The exiled Brutus and Cassius raise an army in Asia Minor and prepare to fight the forces of Antony, Octavius and Lepidus. However, Brutus and Cassius quarrel among themselves. We learn that Portia, Brutus' wife, thinking her husband dead, has committed suicide. Then, in a dream, Brutus sees the Ghost of Caesar, who says they will meet again at Philippi.

Cassius and Brutus take their army to Philippi in Greece. A war between the forces of Cassius and Brutus and the forces of Antony and Octavius will soon begin. On the eve of the battle, the four men meet. Octavius and Antony insult Brutus and Cassius.

In the first stage of the war, the forces of Antony destroy the forces of Cassius, while Brutus' army defeats the army of Octavius. Cassius, fearful of capture, commits suicide. In the second stage of the war, Brutus' army is wiped out, and he commits suicide. Octavius and Antony come upon Brutus' body, and both state he was a worthy enemy, deserving of respect, not hatred.

Detailed Summary of the Play

ACT I
Scene One

The scene as the play opens is a crowded street in Rome. Flavius and Marullus, Tribunes of the People, are trying to send home an unruly mob. The two are officers appointed to protect the common people against the upper classes.

The two Tribunes try to discover why the crowd refuses to leave. They question several workmen, but receive evasive answers. Finally, a shoemaker admits the mob has come to see Julius Caesar in a victory parade.

Marullus loses his temper over the shoemaker's reply. He tells him that Caesar does not deserve a victory parade, for Caesar has defeated Pompey, a former hero of Rome. How can the people, Marullus asks, cheer Caesar whose hands are stained with Pompey's blood. To frighten the crowd into going home, Marullus tells them they will be stricken with disease if they cheer Caesar. Flavius adds the crowd should weep for Pompey into the Tiber—a river running through Rome—until it overflows its banks with tears.

After the crowd disperses, Flavius comments on the common man's ingratitude. He tells Marullus to remove the decorations for the victory parade, but Marullus is scared to do so because the decorations are also being used for a religious festival called the Feast of Lupercal. Flavius says not to be afraid, and to remove the decorations anyway. Before parting, Flavius urges Marullus to send home any other common people he sees on the street, so Caesar will not think the lowly citizens of Rome love and support him.

Scene Two

The victory parade with a large crowd following arrives. In the parade are Caesar, Antony, Calpurnia, Portia, Decius Brutus, Cicero, Cassius and Casca. They are on their way to see a foot race which is run each year on the Feast of Lupercal. During the race, the runners touch any women standing near the raceway because they believe it will cause childless women to have children. Caesar, who is superstitious, tells Antony to touch Calpurnia as he runs by so she will bear a male child. Antony promises to do so.

Suddenly, a Soothsayer (fortune teller) steps out of the crowd and warns Caesar to "Beware the Ides [15th] of March." The Soothsayer repeats his warning at Caesar's request, but Caesar decides to ignore the advice.

After Caesar and the others leave, Cassius and Brutus are left alone. Cassius asks if Brutus is

DETAILED SUMMARY

angry with him, and Brutus replies he is not. Cassius, relieved to hear this answer, tells Brutus how much he likes him, and how worthy a man he himself is.

Cheering is heard from the direction where Caesar went. Brutus says he hopes the people have not made Caesar a king and are cheering for that reason. Cassius exclaims he would rather die than have Caesar rule over him like a dictator. We are equals, Cassius says, so why should Caesar be a master and Cassius a servant. Moreover, Cassius relates how he once saved Caesar's life while swimming, and how Caesar once cried like a woman when he lay ill. Should such a weakling be a king, Cassius asks.

Again, there is cheering. Brutus suspects even more honors are being heaped on Caesar. Cassius begins to flatter Brutus. He tells Brutus that he is more worthy than Caesar, and reminds him that Brutus' ancestor 500 years ago, Lucius Junius Brutus, was famous for overthrowing an unjust king. Cassius hints he is interested in enlisting Brutus in a plot to overthrow Caesar.

Brutus promises to give the overthrow of Caesar further thought. Caesar, looking angry, returns and brings a halt to the conversation. Caesar spies Cassius and tells Antony he does not trust him. Cassius, he says, loves only books and schemes.

DETAILED SUMMARY

When Caesar leaves, Brutus enquires of Casca, who had returned with Caesar's party, the causes of Caesar's anger. Casca explains that Antony offered Caesar a chance to become king three times, but that Caesar turned down the offer each time because he thought the people did not want a monarch. Each time he was offered the crown, however, he was slower about refusing it, because in his heart he really wanted to be king. After Antony offered him the crown the third time, Caesar fainted from epilepsy.

Casca has other news for Brutus. He tells him that Flavius and Marullus have been "silenced" for taking down Caesar's victory decorations. Cassius sees that Casca does not like Caesar, and invites him to dinner where he will try to enlist him into his plot. Brutus leaves Cassius alone, promising to talk further about Caesar.

Cassius speaks out loud. He tells how he will forge letters praising Brutus and damning Caesar for his ambition to become dictator.

Scene Three

It is a stormy evening on the night before the Ides of March. Casca, his sword drawn, is seen running through the streets in terror of the lightning and thunder. Casca meets Cicero,

DETAILED SUMMARY

and tells him that the storm is a warning of a great war to come. Strange things are happening that night, he adds. A slave's hand was plunged into fire but did not burn; a lion walked in the street near the Capitol; owls screeched in the daylight. Cicero, noting Casca's fear, tells him to go home, and departs.

Casca hears footsteps and threatens to stab whoever it is. It is Cassius. He recognizes Casca's voice. After identifying himself, he says that he, too, has heard of strange things happening, but he interprets them as heaven's warning to mankind against Caesar.

Casca says that there are plans afoot to make Caesar king tomorrow in the Capitol. The senators will turn over all of the Roman Empire except Italy to him. Cassius is enraged. Casca says he will join Cassius' plot against Caesar.

As they discuss their plans, Cinna arrives. It becomes apparent that he is part of the conspiracy. The conspiracy has decided to kill Caesar rather than overthrow him. Cassius orders Cinna to place the forged letters where Brutus will find them, for he is almost ready to join them in the plot. Brutus' participation will add respectability to the undertaking.

DETAILED SUMMARY

ACT II

Scene One

Brutus is restlessly pacing his garden. Troubled by indecision over getting rid of Caesar, he cannot sleep. Finally, he decides the only way to prevent Caesar from taking over is to kill him. Lucius, Brutus' servant, enters with one of the forged letters Cinna has planted in the house. It warns of Caesar's power.

There is a knock on the gate. Lucius opens it, and Cassius enters with the other conspirators in the plot: Casca, Decius Brutus, Cinna, Metellus Cimber and Trebonius. All have wrapped their cloaks around their faces so they cannot be recognized. Brutus comments unhappily on how a good deed must be carried out in a sneaky way. To show the others that he fully agrees with their plan to kill Caesar, though, Brutus shakes each of their hands. Cassius suggests they take an oath to kill Caesar, but Brutus says no. Their word as noble Romans is as good as an oath.

Cassius asks that they recruit the respected senator, Cicero, into the plot. Brutus disagrees. Cicero will not follow anyone, Brutus says. Decius Brutus suggests they kill Antony as well, but again Brutus disagrees. He does not want to turn the day into a blood bath.

When the clock strikes three, Trebonius says it is time to go. Cassius warns them Caesar might not show up at the Capitol next day to

DETAILED SUMMARY

meet the senators. Caesar is superstitious, and the storm and strange things happening may keep him away. After discussing this possibility, it is decided that the plotters go to Caesar and escort him to the Capitol.

Before leaving, Metellus Cimber asks that Caius Ligarius be included in the plot. Brutus asks that he interview the man first.

The plotters depart. Brutus calls his servant, but finds him asleep. Brutus, who has not slept since Cassius mentioned the plot, envies his servant. Meanwhile, Portia, Brutus' wife, enters and asks why her husband looks so worried. Brutus does not want to tell her about the plot, but Portia insists he reveal the reason for his concern. Overcome by her devotion, Brutus begins to tell her of the plot. Before he can go into the matter completely, Caius Ligarius arrives for his interview.

Scene Two

The scene changes to Caesar's house on the same stormy night. He, too, cannot sleep. His wife Calpurnia has cried out three times in her sleep that Caesar will be murdered. Caesar decides to sacrifice an animal to the gods and have his fortune told by priests. Calpurnia enters and warns her husband against going out in the morning, for besides her dreams of his death, she has seen a comet. Comets are seen, she reminds her husband, just before the death of kings. Caesar, however, dismisses her fears. A servant enters with news. The priests, after

12

reading Caesar's fortune, say that he should stay home. Caesar ignores their warning: they have read his fortune wrong, he argues. Calpurnia begs him to change his mind. Why not send Antony to the Capitol and have him say Caesar is sick, she suggests. Finally, Caesar gives in and promises not to go out that day.

Just then Decius Brutus arrives. Caesar says he shall not go the Capitol. When Decius Brutus asks why not, Caesar admits with shame it is because of his wife's dreams. Decius Brutus claims Calpurnia's dreams should not be taken as bad omens, and adds that the Senate is anxious to give Caesar the throne. If they think he is a coward, Decius Brutus hints, they may change their mind. The argument persuades Caesar to go out.

Publius, Brutus, Ligarius, Metellus Cimber, Casca, Cinna and Trebonius enter to escort Caesar to the Capitol. Shortly afterwards, Antony arrives. All drink some wine and leave.

Scene Three
Just before Caesar and his escorts arrive at the Capitol, Artemidorus, a teacher of speech, rereads out loud a letter he has written to Caesar warning him of a plot against his life.

Scene Four
Portia sends her servant to the Capitol to check up on things. Brutus has disclosed to her his involvement in the plot. The Soothsayer passes under Portia's window and tells her he is on his way to the Capitol to warn Caesar again.

DETAILED SUMMARY

ACT III
Scene One

As Caesar and his escorts pass through the street, Caesar spies the Soothsayer and reminds him .that the Ides of March have come. But not gone, retorts the Soothsayer. Artemidorus then tries to slip Caesar his warning letter, but Decius Brutus prevents him from doing so by placing a petition in Caesar's hand instead.

Caesar proceeds to the Senate. Popilus, a senator, steps forward and whispers encouragement to Cassius. Cassius, however, is alarmed. He wonders if the plot has been discovered. Popilus, though, says nothing to Caesar.

Trebonius lures Antony away for a chat, leaving Caesar unprotected. As the senators take their seats, the plotters crowd around Caesar. Metellus Cimber begs Caesar to allow a banished brother to return to Rome. Caesar refuses. Others argue in favor of Metellus Cimber's brother, but Caesar will not budge from his decision.

Suddenly, Casca signals the attack, and strikes Caesar with his dagger. One by one, the rest of the plotters do the same. Near death, Caesar sees Brutus raising his dagger and cries, *"Et tu, Brute?"* ("You too, Brutus?") Caesar dies.

As Caesar falls, all the spectators flee in panic. Cinna cries out that liberty has been saved. Cassius urges the others to spread the news of the tyrant's death. Trebonius returns to say that Antony has fled to his home for safety.

Brutus wonders aloud what is in store for the plotters. He suggests that the plotters should dip their arms in Caesar's blood, then go into the market place proclaiming their deed. Cassius remarks that history shall proudly record this day.

As the plotters leave the Senate, Antony's servant arrives. He has a message for them from Antony. It says that Antony is Brutus' friend, and asks why Caesar was killed. Brutus tells the servant to bring Antony to him so he can explain why the plot was hatched. Cassius suspects Antony is up to something and warns Brutus.

Antony arrives and spies Caesar's corpse. Crying out that death is the great leveller, he asks whether the plotters want to kill him too. If so, Antony declares, he is ready. Brutus calms Antony. He tells him that he is welcomed in the plotters' ranks, and will shortly explain why Caesar was assassinated.

Antony pretends to be satisfied, and shakes each plotter's hand. Immediately afterwards, however, he apologizes to Caesar's corpse. Cassius interrupts Brutus. Can we trust you, Antony, he asks. Antony replies they can if they will tell him why it was necessary to kill Caesar. Again, Brutus promises to do just that very soon.

DETAILED SUMMARY

Antony requests he be permitted to deliver the funeral sermon in the market place, and Brutus grants him that favor. Cassius, though, is still suspicious, and again warns Brutus. Brutus replies that he will speak first and tell the people of Rome why Caesar was killed. He also orders Antony to speak only nice things about the plotters. Antony agrees to this condition, and the plotters go off, leaving Brutus alone with Caesar's corpse.

Out of earshot of Caesar's killers, Antony states his true feelings. He asks Caesar (as if he were alive) to forgive what must appear like cowardice. Antony will revenge Caesar's death, he promises, even if it means bloody civil war. As Antony rants on, a servant of Octavius arrives. Antony learns that the dead Caesar's great nephew is on his way to Rome. Antony tells the servant to warn Octavius that Rome is not safe for him. On second thought, says Antony, wait until I have delivered the funeral sermon, and I can gauge the crowd's reaction. Antony and the servant carry off Caesar's body.

Scene Two

The same afternoon, a mob gathers in the market place. When Brutus and Cassius arrive, the mob angrily demands an explanation. Brutus divides the mob in two: he sends one half to listen to Cassius' explanation and urges the other half to remain and hear his.

Brutus' speech is clear, logical and unemotional. The listeners are not overly enthusiastic. Then

17

DETAILED SUMMARY

Antony appears with Caesar's body. Brutus introduces Antony, saying that he would commit suicide himself if he had not acted wisely in killing Caesar. The crowd finally cheers Brutus at this point. Brutus departs, begging the audience to remain and hear Antony's funeral sermon.

Antony climbs to the pulpit amidst threatening whispers. He better not say anything against Brutus, says one person. Finally, Antony begins his famous speech, "Friends, Romans, and countrymen, lend me your ears...." He tells the audience he came only to bury Caesar, not to praise him. He did not know, Antony continues, that Caesar was so ambitious to become a dictator, but it must be so if Brutus says Caesar was. For Brutus is an "honorable man," and therefore tells only the truth.

The audience soon discovers that Antony is being sarcastic when he calls Brutus an "honorable man." In a short time, the audience begins muttering threats against Brutus, and saying how wonderful Caesar was. Antony begins to cry. When he stops, Antony apologizes for making the audience angry at Brutus and the plotters. He takes Caesar's will from his cloak, but says he cannot read it because the people would love Caesar too much if they knew what he had left them. The curious audience shouts for Antony to read it anyway. No, answers Antony, for they would see how much Caesar loved them.

DETAILED SUMMARY

The audience goes wild with curiosity (as Antony intended), and begs Antony to read the will. But, it might make the audience angry with Brutus and the plotters, says Antony, and they are "honorable men." No, they aren't "honorable men," someone in the audience shouts. They're murderers! Read the will!

Antony consents to read it finally, but tells the audience to gather round the corpse while he does so. Antony descends from the pulpit to join them.

Antony lifts Caesar's cloak without revealing the body. He shows the horrified audience where each plotter's dagger tore through the garment, and makes sarcastic remarks about the murderers. Soon, Antony calls Caesar's assassination high treason. The audience is deeply moved. Just as they reach the fever pitch of grief, Antony rips away Caesar's cloak completely so that the audience may actually see the bloody body. The audience is shocked.

Antony shouts that the plotters are traitors. The audience cries out for revenge. Hold on a moment, Antony asks. He apologizes to them that he is a poor speaker (when in fact he is an excellent speaker), but says that Caesar's wounds speak for themselves. The audience is enraged again and wants to kill Brutus. Again, Antony asks that they be patient for a few minutes so he can read them the will which they've forgotten all about.

DETAILED SUMMARY

Caesar's will, the audience discovers, gives each of them a sum of money. In addition, it bequeathes to the city of Rome Caesar's private gardens and orchids.

The audience gets out of control. They tear up all the wooden furniture in sight to make a funeral pyre to cremate Caesar's corpse. Antony watches the scene with satisfaction. He has succeeded in whipping the audience into a frenzy.

A servant enters and announces Octavius' arrival in Rome. He is waiting with the famous soldier Lepidus at Caesar's house. Antony tells the servant he will join them shortly. The servant also reports that Cassius and Brutus have fled Rome. Antony is overjoyed and departs for Caesar's house.

Scene Three

Mobs are looting and burning after Antony's speech. The poet Cinna (not the plotter) is strolling down the street on his way to Caesar's funeral. Suddenly, he meets a small mob. They mistake him for Cinna the plotter and threaten to kill him. He protests that they are making a mistake. So what, cries one of the mob, and Cinna is ruthlessly murdered. The mob then goes off to burn the house of one of the plotters.

DETAILED SUMMARY
ACT IV
Scene One

Antony, Octavius and Lepidus are holding a meeting in Antony's house. Decisions are being made as to who will die in a purge of Brutus' supporters. Octavius informs Lepidus that Lepidus' own brother must die. Lepidus agrees to this only if Antony's nephew, another supporter of Brutus, will be executed too. Antony calmly consents. Later, Antony sends Lepidus for Caesar's will to see if any of Caesar's heirs named in the document can be "removed."

The minute Lepidus is out of sight, Antony tells Octavius that Lepidus is worthless and does not deserve to share power with them. Octavius replies that Antony sought Lepidus' advice on whom to put on the list of victims. Antony explains that he was just setting Lepidus up to take the blame, as the relatives of the executed men would think it was all Lepidus' doing. Antony then tells Octavius that Brutus and Cassius have raised an army and are preparing for war. We must do likewise, Antony concludes.

Scene Two

It is a month or two later. Brutus and Cassius' armies have joined up near Sardis, a city in Asia Minor. Both men are preparing to wage civil war against Octavius and Antony. However, on meeting one another, Cassius and

DETAILED SUMMARY

Brutus start a violent argument. Rather than allow their soldiers to overhear, Brutus invites Cassius into his tent to continue the quarrel.

Scene Three

Cassius complains that Brutus has punished one of his officers too harshly for taking a bribe. Brutus retorts that Cassius is more interested in money than war. The argument heats up, each claiming to be a better general. Soon, however, Cassius is upset to see their friendship deteriorating so, and tries to make up. Brutus and Cassius shake hands. Immediately afterwards, a silly poet rushes into the tent to restore the friendship.

Brutus reveals he has heard of Portia's death by suicide. Then, scouts arrive with news of the approach of Antony and Octavius to Philippi in northern Greece. Cassius urges Brutus that they await Octavius and Antony where they are. Brutus disagrees: he wants to go to Philippi to meet the enemy.

Cassius leaves, but Brutus is unable to sleep. His servant Lucius plays him a song upon a lute to calm him, but it does not work. Brutus decides to read a while. Suddenly, Caesar's Ghost appears before him. Brutus is terrified. Caesar's Ghost threatens to meet him again at Philippi, then disappears. Brutus immediately questions the guards at the tent's entrance, but they have seen nothing.

DETAILED SUMMARY
ACT V
Scene One

Octavius and Antony are standing above the plains of Philippi. They are delighted to see the armies of Brutus and Cassius approach below because their height in the hills gives them a military advantage.

Before the battle, the four generals—Antony, Octavius, Brutus and Cassius—meet for preliminary discussions. The meeting turns into an insult hurling affair. Antony and Octavius call Brutus and Cassius traitors. The four men separate and return to their armies.

Back in camp, Cassius complains that he has seen bad omens. Vultures have followed his armies. Cassius also reveals that this day is his birthday. Frightened that the armies of Brutus and himself might lose, he suggests making a suicide pact with Brutus. Brutus refuses, although he swears he will not be taken a prisoner to Rome.

Scene Two

The battle starts with loud fanfare. Brutus' army moves swiftly against Octavius' army, and soon gets the upper hand.

Scene Three

Cassius' army, however, is not as fortunate as the army of Brutus. Antony's troops easily fight them off. Cassius needs the aid of Brutus' army, but they are too busy taking care of their dead and looting.

The battlefield is a scene of wild confusion, and Cassius calls for a retreat. Later, Cassius sees troops approaching, but they are so distant he cannot identify them. He sends his lieutenant Titinius to discover who they are. Still unable to identify them so far away, Cassius watches as they seem to surround Titinius. They must be enemy troops, Cassius concludes. All is lost. Cassius orders a servant to kill him with the very dagger he used to stab Caesar.

Seconds later, Titinius returns escorted by some of Brutus' men. It was they, not the enemy, Cassius had seen surround his lieutenant. Discovering the body of Cassius, Titinius also commits suicide with Cassius' dagger.

Brutus arrives shortly afterwards, and delivers the funeral service for his two friends.

Scene Four

The armies of Antony and Octavius quickly recover from the drubbing Brutus' army inflicted on them, and go back into battle. Brutus' men fight hard and gallantly, but when one of his top officers, Young Cato, is killed, and another officer, Lucilius, is captured, the battle is lost.

DETAILED SUMMARY

Scene Five

As the armies of Antony and Octavius approach for the kill, Brutus and a few of his officers go off to a hilltop. Brutus asks two of his men to kill him, but they refuse. When the enemy is almost on them, the officers flee for their lives, leaving only Brutus and Strato, a former slave. Strato, at Brutus' request, holds Brutus' sword as his general runs upon it and kills himself.

Shortly afterwards, Antony and Octavius reach the hilltop. They spy the body of Brutus, and enquire of Strato the identity of the corpse. Strato tells them it is Brutus, and asks that the dead man be given a respectful burial. Octavius and Antony agree to do so. Antony looks down on Brutus and exclaims, "This was the noblest Roman of them all. . . ."

Sketches of the
Major Characters

JULIUS CAESAR: There are two portraits of Caesar in this play: the living Caesar and the dead Caesar. While alive, Caesar is an intense human being. He is conceited, arrogant, foolish, superstitious, tender, cruel and concerned with his health. In short, he could be anyone.

After his assassination, however, we see Caesar in a new light. Through his will, we discover him to be a towering political figure, a courageous soldier and kindly leader. He has dominated and transformed Rome for the better through sheer will and energy. His death cannot alter his effect on history.

BRUTUS: Brutus, like Caesar, is a hero. He is not, though, a powerful and decisive man like Caesar. An intellectual, he is tormented by the conflict within him of love for Caesar and love for liberty, which he suspects Caesar will destroy. Brutus is also naive, and it is easy for Cassius to flatter him and draw him into the conspiracy. His immaturity permits the plotters to attach Brutus' good name to a foul deed.

CASSIUS: The instigator of the assassination, Cassius is motivated more by his hatred of Caesar than his love of freedom. Yet, Cassius is also somewhat indecisive. For example, he permits Brutus to persuade him against his better judgment to allow Antony to deliver the funeral oration.

26

MARC ANTONY: Like Caesar, there are two sides to Antony in this play. At first, the audience sees him as a passionate youth, more interested in sowing his wild oats than in art or philosophy. Upon Caesar's death, however, a new Antony emerges. His funeral oration, which turns the citizens of Rome against the conspirators, is a masterpiece of subtlety and cunning. In addition, the audience soon discovers how ruthless and politically ambitious Antony really is. Yet, if we fault him for his ambition and cruelty, we must praise him for his valor and loyalty to Caesar. For in his devotion to Caesar, he is as sincere as Brutus in his devotion to liberty.

CALPURNIA: Caesar's wife, like her husband, is portrayed as a real human being, full of hopes and fears. Her main function in the play is to try to prevent Caesar from going to meet his death. Through her, Shakespeare created *dramatic tension.*

PORTIA: The wife of Brutus differs from Calpurnia in many ways. Daughter of a famous nobleman and philosopher named Cato, she is less superstitious and more intellectual. Her husband can confide in her, for she understands the depth of Brutus' problem when he is brooding about joining the plot to murder Caesar. She commits suicide when Brutus is forced to flee from Rome after Marc Antony's funeral speech.

27

Sources for *Julius Caesar*

Shakespeare, it is obvious, based his play upon real characters from history. To find out about the "historical" Roman figures such as Brutus, Caesar, Octavius, Antony and others, Shakespeare consulted the following books:

1. *The Lives of the Noble Grecians and Romans.* This famous collection of biographies by the great Roman writer Plutarch appeared in England in 1579 after being translated by Sir Thomas North from a French edition. Although Shakespeare drew heavily on the characterization of such famous people as Caesar, Brutus, Octavius, Antony and others, he did change a number of Plutarch's details in order to make his play more dramatic.

2. Besides reading Plutarch, Shakespeare probably used the books of Appian, a Roman historian, in order to learn more about the history of Rome and the central characters in his play. For example, the Antony in Shakespeare's *Julius Caesar* more closely resembles Appian's than Plutarch's account of him.

3. In addition to Plutarch and Appian, Shakespeare knew about Roman history from a number of books on philosophy and from other contemporary sources.

BRIEF BIOGRAPHY OF WILLIAM SHAKESPEARE

Few verifiable facts are known about William Shakespeare's life. Scholars since the eighteenth century have hunted regularly through texts, accounts, and folios to unearth more information about this greatest of English dramatists, and only in the twentieth century have any new "clues" come to light. Even these afford little more than speculation, as in the case of a recent study by A.L. Rowse (which has been criticized for inaccuracies) based on his investigation of certain royal household records and of receipts and records of the Globe Theatre.

Partially because of this paucity of knowledge, which seems to have been the case even during Shakespeare's life, many people —even among his contemporaries—believed "William Shakespeare" was a pseudonym for some famous person. Among those "suspected" were Christopher Marlowe (who was born in the same year as Shakespeare), Francis Bacon, the Earl of Oxford, Sir Philip Sydney, and Queen Elizabeth herself. Some of these "cults" are still active and are responsible for an enormous amount of Shakespearian fact-hunting. Others since the seventeenth century have believed that the William Shakespeare of Stratford-on-Avon wrote the plays and poems, but they have been at pains to decipher from the works the identities of Shakespeare's acquaintances. One of the more interesting of these works is Oscar Wilde's *Portrait of Mr. W.M.,* in which Wilde attempts to identify the beloved man ("W.H."), and the "dark lady" of the sonnets.

Finally, most scholars agree that because the folios were made up *after* Shakespeare's death, and were apparently taken from actors' copies, many errors and misreadings were incorporated. Further, because Heminges and Condell published the plays as an act of tribute, and because it is likely that they were unfamiliar with all of Shakespeare's work, we not only probably lack certain writings, but we also (almost definitely) have non-Shakespearian material included. The new Riverside Edition of the complete plays, edited by Professor G. Blakemore Evans, will be of interest to anyone who wishes to study textual changes and differences.

William Shakespeare was born about April 22, 1564 to Mary and John Shakespeare of Stratford-on-Avon, and he was baptised on April 26 of that year. His father, apparently a wealthy merchant, later became mayor and was knighted in 1596. In 1582, when he was 18, Shakespeare was granted a license to marry Anne Hathaway, a woman eight years older than himself. A daughter, Susanna, was born to them six months later. In 1585, twins were born to them, named Judith and Hamnet. The following year, Shakespeare left Stratford-on-Avon for London. It is not known if his family accompanied him.

In 1592, the author and journalist Robert Greene, in a satirical essay about dramatists in London, angrily attacked Shakespeare in print. It is the first open reference to him as a playwright. In 1593, the year of a plague that decimated London, Shakespeare published a long poem, *Venus and Adonis.* He published *The Rape of Lucrece,* another long poem, in 1594, and subsequently his name appears on the roles of the Lord Chamberlain's Men (later The King's Men), a noted theatrical company, for that year.

Shakespeare's son Hamnet died in 1595, and apparently his entire family was with him in London at that time. Although remaining in residence in London. Shakespeare bought the most expensive house in Stratford in 1597, called New Place, and in the following year the critic Francis Meres wrote a long praise of Shakespeare's work, mentioning the author's poems, sonnets, and twelve plays. In 1603, after Queen Elizabeth's death, Shakespeare and his fellow players, now housed in their own Globe Theatre, of which Shakespeare was part owner, received honors from James I and became Grooms of the King's Chamber.

Shakespeare's daughter Susanna married in 1607. The following year, his mother died, following his father by seven years. In 1609 he published the sonnets, and one year later he retired to New Place, where he lived for the rest of his life. In 1616, the same year of the marriage of his other daughter Judith, William Shakespeare died in Stratford. Seven years later, in 1623, Heminges and Condell brought out the first folio edition of his plays.

WORKS OF SHAKESPEARE

Because scholars disagree as to when Shakespeare wrote his plays, the dates of composition given are only approximations. The letters (H), (C) and (T) indicate whether the play is a historical drama, comedy or tragedy.

Apprenticeship (1590-1594)

1590   *The Comedy of Errors* (C).

1591   *Two Gentlemen of Verona* (C), *Love's Labour's Lost* (C), *Henry VI Part I, Henry VI Part II, Henry VI Part III* (H or T).

1592/93 *Titus Andronicus* (T), *Richard III* (H or T).

Great Histories and Comedies (1595-1600)

1595   *A Midsummer Night's Dream* (C), *Richard II* (H or T), *Romeo and Juliet* (T).

1596   *The Merchant of Venice* (C), *King John* (H or T).

1597   *Henry IV Part I, Henry IV Part II* (H), *Much Ado About Nothing* (C).

1598   *The Taming of the Shrew* (C), *The Merry Wives of Windsor* (C).

1599   *Henry V* (H), *Julius Caesar* (T).

1600   *As You Like It* (C), *Twelfth Night* (C).

Tragi-Comedies and Great Tragedies (1601-1613)

1601   *Hamlet* (T), *All's Well That Ends Well* (C).

1602   *Troilus and Cressida* (C), *Measure for Measure* (C).

1604   *Othello* (T).

1605   *King Lear* (T), *Timon of Athens* (T).

1606   *Macbeth* (T), *Antony and Cleopatra* (T).

1607/08 *Pericles, Prince of Tyre* (C), *Coriolanus* (T).

1609   *Sonnets* (published), *Cymbeline* (C).

1610   *The Winter's Tale* (C), *The Tempest* (C).

1613   *Henry VIII* (H).

THE THEATER IN
SHAKESPEARE'S TIME

TYPES OF THEATERS: The two main types were *public* and *private*. Although the interiors were similar, the public theater was *round* and *unroofed,* while the private was *square* and *roofed.* Each was three stories high, each story corresponding to the three galleries inside. As there were no seats, the audience stood. Admission to the pit in public theaters ran about one cent. The pit is similar to our modern orchestra. As the public theaters were not roofed and used natural light instead of torches, all performances were given in the afternoon. The famous Globe Theater, in which Shakespeare produced most of his plays, was a public theater.

SHAPE OF THE STAGE AREA: The Globe theater had a *main stage,* about 40 feet wide and projecting 27 feet into the pit. It was used mainly for outdoor scenes and mass effects.

Directly behind the main stage was the *first inner stage,* hidden by a curtain. This was used for interior scenes.

Above the first inner stage was a *second inner stage,* with curtains and a balcony. This was used for window or wall scenes.

Above the second inner stage was a *music room* for musicians. Occasionally, it was used for dramatic action in high window or wall scenes.

At the very top of the stage roof was the *"huts,"* a structure containing hoists to raise actors and props. On days of the performance, a flag was flown from a turret that protruded above the open roof of the theater.

SCENERY AND COSTUMES: Although there were no stage sets in the modern sense, heavy props and decorated curtains made for elaborate sets. The costumes worn were luxurious and striking.

EFFECTS OF THE STAGE ON SHAKESPEARE'S PLAYS: Because the stage was in full view of the audience and lacked wings, many rapid changes of scene occur in Shakespeare's plays.

At the same time, because the stage jutted out into the audience, it was customary for the actors to make long speeches directly to the audience.

Because there was no modern lighting, it was necessary for the characters in the play to make reference to time, season and weather so the audience could understand what time the action occurred.

Knowing that he had to appeal to all types of audiences—the poor people in the pits and the upper classes in the more expensive balconies—Shakespeare wrote scenes that would be appreciated by his entire audience. In many plays, the playwright combined low comedy with high tragedy.

IMPORTANT DATES
IN ENGLISH HISTORY
FOR STUDENTS OF
SHAKESPEARE

1485   Henry VII (Tudor) defeats Richard III (York) at Bosworth and ends the 30-year civil war called War of the Roses. Henry VII established a strong monarchy over England.

1534   Henry VIII, Henry VII's son, breaks with the Roman Catholic Church, and increases King's rule over the country by using tyrannical means.

1547   Death of Henry VIII.

1553   Henry VIII's daughter, Mary, tries to bring back the Roman Catholic Church, causing strife and rebellion among the Protestants of England.

1558   Queen Elizabeth, another daughter of Henry VIII, comes to the throne. Only 25 years old, she establishes the Protestant Church of England, encourages industry and art.

Shakespeare's first history plays praise the Tudor family directly, which flatters Elizabeth.

1587   Queen Elizabeth has Mary executed. Sir Walter Raleigh establishes colony in the New World (Virginia). Elizabethans fascinated with tales of discovery and exploration. Trade and commerce stimulated.

1588   Sir Francis Drake defeats the Spanish Armada, establishes England as mistress of the seas and the most powerful nation in the world. Throughout the remainder of Elizabeth's reign, England's literature glorifies patriotism and love of country.

Though Queen of England, Elizabeth has many enemies in her own country who would like to see her removed from the throne. These enemies are generally from the upper classes. The common people, workers and merchants, love their ruler.

1603   Death of childless Queen Elizabeth.

James VI of Scotland (Stuart) comes to the throne as James I. Less tolerant and wise than Queen Elizabeth, James I is hated by many for his tyrannical behavior.

Despite his unpopularity, James I did encourage art. The "English Renaissance," started in Elizabeth's time, continued. Writers like Shakespeare, Ben Jonson and Milton flourished. James I, too, initiated the writing of the King James version of the Bible.

IMPORTANT DATES IN ROMAN HISTORY FOR STUDENTS OF *JULIUS CAESAR*

The student should remember that Shakespeare "rewrote" history in his play *Julius Caesar* whenever he thought it would be more dramatic to alter actual events. These important dates should be compared to what happened in the play.

B.C.

60   To end possible civil war between supporters of the Senate and its enemies, Caesar establishes a three man committee to rule Rome: Pompey, Crassus, and himself. In theory, if not in fact, this committee was under the final authority of the Senate.

49   Caesar defies the Senate by bringing his army back from the wars in Gaul. He crosses the Rubicon river north of Rome to take over the city. Bitter fighting breaks out between his armies and supporters of the Senate.

48   The supporters of the Senate send Pompey to fight Caesar at Pharsalus, but Caesar easily defeats Pompey's forces. Afterwards, he pursues Pompey to Egypt in order to finish him off, but discovers Pompey has died before his arrival. Caesar begins a liaison with Cleopatra.

45 Caesar defeats Pompey's sons in the battle of Munda, Spain. The sons are killed. Caesar returns to Rome and establishes himself as dictator.

44 Caesar assassinated on the Ides (15th) of March.

43–42 Octavius (the grandnephew of Caesar who took the name Caesar Octavian), Marc Antony and Lepidus form another three-man committee to rule Rome. They defeat the armies of Brutus at Philippi. Lepidus is stripped of power, after which Octavian and Marc Antony divide the Roman Empire between them, Octavian to rule in the West, Marc Antony in the East. Antony falls in love with Cleopatra.

31 In a bid for sole power and control, Octavian declares war on Antony, and defeats Antony's army at Actium on the west coast of Greece. Marc Antony and Cleopatra commit suicide.

27–14 As sole ruler of Rome, Octavian, now called Augustus, promotes peace, prosperity and a rebirth of art (called by historians The Golden Age of Rome or The Augustan Age).

ESSENTIAL ANNOTATED BIBLIOGRAPHY

For class discussion, term papers and book reports, the student will find the following books extremely helpful. Titles with an asterisk (*) may be bought in inexpensive paperback editions.

Life of Shakespeare

Alexander, P., *Shakespeare's Life and Art*. New York: N.Y.U. Press, 1961. Traces Shakespeare's development as a playwright.

Chute, Marchette. *Shakespeare of London*. New York: Dutton, 1949. A clear, complete biography, and an excellent portrait of the times.

Fluchere, Henri. *Shakespeare and the Elizabethans*. New York: Hill and Wang, 1956. A comparative study of Shakespeare and other playwrights of the period.

Van Doren, Mark. *Shakespeare**. New York: Doubleday, 1955 (first printed 1941). A good biography of Shakespeare for beginners.

Shakespeare's Times

Baugh, A. C., *A Literary History of Eng-*

land. New York: Appleton-Century-Crofts, 1948. The best reference book on the history of English literature.

Tillyard, E. M. W., *The Elizabethan World Picture*. London: Chatto & Windus, 1943. The best study of the Elizabethan's outlook on the world around him.

Trevelyan, G. M., *History of England, Volume II: The Tudors and the Stuart Era**. New York: Doubleday, 1956 (first printed 1926). Besides this book's wealth of information, it it written in lively, clear and concise prose.

Wilson, John D., *Life in Shakespeare's England**. Baltimore: Penguin Books, 1959. A fascinating description of life on all levels of Elizabethan society.

The Theater of Shakespeare's Times

Adams, John C., *The Globe Playhouse: Its Design and Equipment*. New York: Barnes and Noble, 1961. Excellent book on the theater Shakespeare owned and wrote for.

Chambers, E. K., *The Elizabethan Stage*. Oxford: The University Press, 1923. Four vols. The classic study of Shakespearean production, but slightly advanced for younger students.

HISTORICAL SOURCES FOR *JULIUS CAESAR*

MacCallum, M. W., *Shakespeare's Roman Plays and Their Background*. New York: Macmillan, 1910. Out-of-date, but still useful book on Shakespeare's sources for his Roman plays.

Palmer, John, *Political Characters in Shakespeare**. New York: St. Martin's Press, 1945. Provides an excellent understanding of political background for *Julius Caesar*.

Plutarch, *Lives of Coriolanus, Caesar, Brutus, and Antonius*. (Edited by R. H. Carr.) Oxford: The University Press, 1938. A lively, clear text of the accepted source of *Julius Caesar*.

GENERAL WORKS ON *JULIUS CAESAR*

Bonjour, Adrien, *The Structure of Julius Caesar*. Liverpool: University Press of Liverpool, 1958. An excellent study of the dramatic construction of Shakespeare's play.

Kittredge, George Lyman, ed., *Julius Caesar**. London: Ginn and Company, 1939. The best edition of the play. Contains an excellent introduction and analysis by one of the world's great Shakespeare authorities.

Knight, G. Wilson, *The Imperial Theme*, New York: British Book Center, 1951. An important discussion of the Elizabethan conception of power and monarchs.